PASTRIES & BAKING

PASTRIES & BAKING

Delicious teatime treats, from classic
breads to fancy pastries

CONTENTS

TECHNIQUES 6

RECIPES 12
Ficelles 12
Seven-grain bread 14
Walnut bread 16
Plaited loaf 18
Brioche 20
Focaccia 22
Crusty white loaf 24
Morning rolls 26
Sourdough bread with fennel seeds 28
Crumpets 30
Wholemeal bread 32
Ciabatta 34
Onion and herb loaf 36
English muffins 38
Spiced fruit buns 40
Rye bread 42
Croissants 44
Chapatis 46
Pitta bread 48
Naan bread 50
Moroccan spiced flatbreads 52
Scotch pancakes 54
Waffles 56
Scones 58
Mini chocolate nut pastries 60

Mini chocolate éclairs 62
Silesian poppy tart 64
Pecan pie 66
Blueberry cream cheese tart 68
Banana cream pie 70
Apple pie 72
Key lime pie 74
Lemon tart 76
Lemon meringue pie 78
Cannoli 80
Profiteroles 82
Pear and cinnamon strudel 84
Crème pâtissière 86
Florentines 88
Spritzgebäck biscuits 90
Rich chocolate biscuits 92

INDEX 94
ACKNOWLEDGMENTS 96

Guide to symbols

The recipes in this book are accompanied by symbols that alert you to important information.

 Tells you how many people the recipe serves, or how much is produced.

 Indicates how much time you will need to prepare and cook a dish. Next to this symbol you will also find out if additional time is required for such things as marinating, standing, proving, or cooling. You need to read the recipe to find out exactly how much extra time is needed.

 Alerts you to what has to be done before you can begin to cook the recipe, or to parts of the recipe that take a long time to complete.

 Denotes that special equipment is required. Where possible, alternatives are given.

 Accompanies freezing information.

Techniques

Mix and knead yeast dough
Dough should be well combined and kneaded to a silken and elastic finish

1 Place the dry ingredients in a large bowl and gradually add the liquid ingredients. Combine using your fingers, digging into the bottom of the bowl and pressing the dough through your fingers to mix.

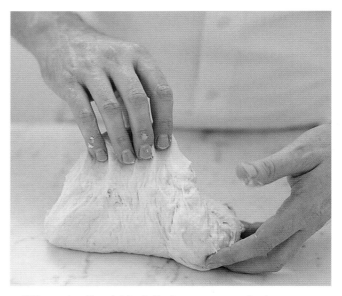

2 When the liquid is fully incorporated, the dough should be soft but not sticky. When ready to knead, turn the dough out on to a floured surface and, with oiled fingers, fold it in half towards you.

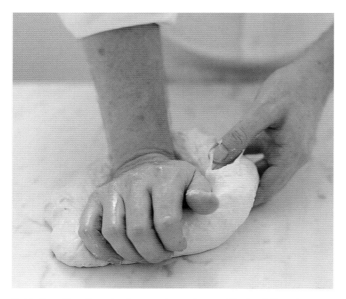

3 Using the heel of your hand, gently but firmly press down and away through the centre to stretch and knead the dough. Lift and rotate the dough a quarter turn.

4 Repeat the folding, pressing and rotating 10–12 times. Let the dough rest, as directed in your recipe, then continue kneading. Each kneading will require less oil and produce a more elastic dough.

Make brioche dough

This dough is very sticky so it is easier to make using an electric mixer. See p20 for ingredient quantities.

1 Pour the dry ingredients into the bowl of the mixer. Using the dough hook attachment, mix on medium speed and add the milk and eggs a little at a time. Mix until smooth and fully incorporated.

2 Once the dough is mixed and begins to come away from the edges of the bowl, add butter (at room temperature and cut into pieces). Mix again until the dough comes away from the edges.

3 When the dough is mixed, transfer it to another large bowl. Cover with cling film and leave it to sit at room temperature for 2–3 hours, or until it doubles in size. The risen dough will be very sticky.

4 Lightly flour a work surface and punch down the dough with your fist to deflate it. Return it to the bowl, cover with cling film, and chill to let it rise for 1¼ hours. Deflate once more, then shape and bake.

Make pastry

Once rested, pastry dough can be used at once or stored for up to two days in a refrigerator, wrapped in cling film. This recipes makes 1kg (2¼lb) of pastry.

1 Mix 375g (13 oz) unsalted, softened butter, with 1 egg yolk and 1½ teaspoons of salt. In another bowl, mix 2 teaspoons of sugar with 100ml (3½fl oz) milk, then gradually stir it into the butter mixture.

2 Sift 500g (1lb 2oz) of plain flour into a bowl, then gradually stir it into the butter. When all the flour is added, continue mixing with a wooden spoon or gently combine with your hands.

3 Dust a work surface with flour and turn out the pastry. Using the palm of your hand, lightly knead the pastry until it forms a soft, moist dough.

4 Shape the dough into a ball, wrap it in cling film, and refrigerate for at least 2 hours. Allowing the gluten and flour to relax during chilling will prevent the dough from shrinking when in the hot oven.

Bake pastry blind

A pastry case for a tart or pie must be pre-cooked if its filling will not be baked or baked only for a short time.

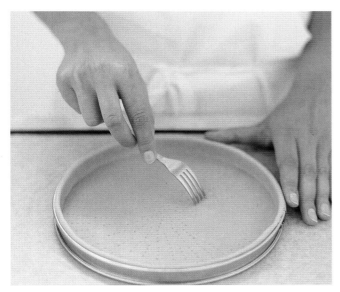

1 Once the pastry is fitted in the tin, prick the bottom with a fork. This will allow trapped air to escape during baking.

2 Cut out a circle of baking parchment, just slightly larger than the tin. Fold the parchment in half 3 times to make a triangular shape and clip the edges at regular intervals with scissors.

3 Place the parchment circle into the tin and fill it with an even layer of ceramic or metal baking beans. Bake at 180°C (350°F/ Gas 4) for 15–20 minutes – it will be partially baked.

4 When cool enough to handle, remove the beans and parchment. For fully baked pastry, return the pastry to the oven for a further 5–8 minutes, or until golden.

Trim and decorate pastry

Before baking pies and tarts, remove excess pastry, and decorate the edges for a finished look.

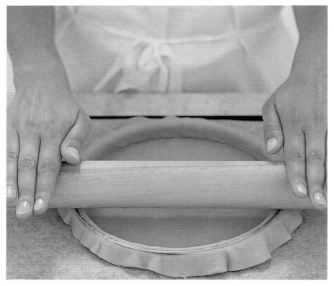

Trim: Roll the pastry out, then press it gently into the bottom of the tin and against the sides. Firmly roll a rolling pin over the top of the tin to trim off the excess pastry.

Forked edge: Using a fork, press the dough to the rim of the plate. Repeat around the edge in even intervals.

Rope edge: Pinch the dough between your thumb and the knuckle of your index finger, then place your thumb in the groove left by the index finger and pinch as before. Repeat around the edge.

Fluted edge: Push one index finger against the outside edge of the rim and pinch the pastry with the other index finger and thumb to form a ruffle. Repeat around the edge, leaving an even gap between each ruffle.

Whip cream

Chill the whisk, bowl, and cream beforehand, but remove the cream from the refrigerator and let it reach 5°C (40°F) before whipping.

1 Start whipping slowly with about 2 strokes per second (or the lowest speed on an electric mixer) until the cream begins to thicken.

2 Increase to a moderate speed for soft peaks. For stiff peaks, continue beating and test by lifting the beaters to see if the cream retains its shape.

Pipe

For more than just cream, a bag and nozzle can be used to pipe meringue, pastry, and sorbet.

1 Place the nozzle in the bag and twist to seal. Hold the bag just above the nozzle, fold the top of the bag over to create a "collar", and spoon in the filling. Continue until the bag is three-quarters full.

2 Twist the top of the bag to close and expel any air. Holding the twisted end taut in one hand, use your other hand to gently press the filling to start a steady flow and direct the nozzle as desired.

Ficelles

These are very thin baguettes with a light, crisp crust.

INGREDIENTS

500g (1lb 2oz) strong plain flour
4 tsp salt
7g sachet fast-action dried yeast
150ml (5fl oz) boiling water

METHOD

1 Place the flour, 1 teaspoon of the salt, and the yeast in a bowl. Add 350ml (12fl oz) of tepid water and mix into a dough. Knead the dough on a lightly floured surface for 10 minutes.

2 Divide the dough into 4 and roll each into a 30cm (12in) long baguette shape. Slash diagonally with a sharp knife. Cover loosely and leave in a warm place for 1 hour, or until doubled in size.

3 Preheat the oven to 220°C (425°F/Gas 7). Dissolve the remaining salt in the boiling water. Brush over the loaves and bake for 15–20 minutes, or until they are a light golden colour.

4 Remove from the oven and slide on to a wire rack to cool. Serve warm, with lots of butter.

makes 4 loaves

**prep 15 mins,
plus rising
• cook 15–20 mins**

Seven-grain bread

INGREDIENTS

85g (3 oz) bulgur wheat
50g (1¾ oz) polenta
50g (1¾ oz) millet
50g (1¾ oz) quinoa
450g (1lb) strong white flour
250g (9 oz) granary flour or
  strong wholemeal flour
75g (2½ oz) rolled oats
75g (2½ oz) rye flakes
2 x 7g sachets easy-blend dried yeast

2 tsp salt
50g (1¾ oz) cooked long-grain
  brown rice
4 tbsp honey, maple syrup, or treacle,
  to taste
250ml (9fl oz) milk, warmed
2 tbsp sunflower oil, plus extra
  for brushing
600ml (1 pint) water, warmed

METHOD

1 Put the first 4 ingredients into a heatproof bowl. Pour over 400ml (14fl oz) of water, stir, cover with a folded tea towel, and leave to stand for 15 minutes.

2 Put the next 6 ingredients into a separate bowl and combine well. Tip in the bulgur wheat mixture with any remaining water, add the brown rice, and stir.

3 Heat the honey and milk in a saucepan over a low heat until the honey dissolves. Add the milk mixture and the sunflower oil to the flour mixture and stir together. Gradually add up to 200ml (7fl oz) water, or until a soft, sticky dough forms. Dust a work surface with flour, turn out the dough, and knead for 10 minutes, or until elastic, adding extra flour as necessary.

4 Rub the inside of a dry bowl with sunflower oil. Shape the dough into a ball and lightly coat the ball with oil by turning it within the bowl. Cover the bowl with cling film and set aside in a warm, draught-free place until the dough doubles in size. Grease and flour the loaf tins.

5 Once risen, punch down the dough, turn out on to a floured surface and knead for 1 minute. (The dough will be sticky again.) Cut the dough into 2 equal-sized balls and use a floured rolling pin to roll each ball into a rectangle as wide as the tins and twice as long. Fold both ends to the centre and pinch the edges to seal. Place the dough in the tins, cover with tea towels, and set aside to rise until the dough reaches the tops of the tins. Meanwhile, preheat the oven to 220°C (425°F/Gas 7).

6 When the dough has risen, brush the tops with sunflower oil. Bake for 10 minutes, then reduce the heat to 190°C (375°F/Gas 5) for a further 25–30 minutes, or until the loaves sound hollow when tapped on the base. If not, return to the oven for 5–10 minutes.

makes 2 loaves

prep 20 mins, plus standing and rising • cook 35–40 mins

2 × 900g (2lb) loaf tins

freeze for up to 3 months

Walnut bread

In France, this savoury bread is a traditional accompaniment to the cheese course.

INGREDIENTS

350g (12 oz) strong wholemeal flour
200g (7 oz) strong white flour, plus extra
  for dusting
7g sachet easy-blend dried yeast
1½ tsp salt
1 tsp sugar
1 tbsp walnut oil, plus extra for brushing
150g (5½oz) walnuts, coarsely chopped

METHOD

1 Mix the first 5 ingredients in a large bowl, making a well in the centre. Stir 350ml (12fl oz) tepid water and the walnut oil into the well. Gradually add up to 100ml (3½fl oz) more water until the flour is incorporated and the dough is soft.

2 Turn out the dough on to a lightly floured surface and knead for 5–8 minutes, or until smooth and elastic. Shape into a ball.

3 Rub the inside of a dry bowl with oil. Put the dough in the bowl, cover with cling film, and leave in a warm place until doubled in size. Meanwhile, lightly dust a large baking tray with flour.

4 Punch down the dough, turn it out on to a floured surface, and knead for 1 minute. Pat the dough into a rectangle and sprinkle with the walnuts. Knead for a few more minutes, or until the nuts are evenly distributed.

5 Cut the dough in half and form each into a ball. Transfer to the baking tray and flatten. Cover with a tea towel and leave to rise for 15 minutes. Preheat the oven to 220°C (425°F/Gas 7).

6 Lightly dust the dough with flour, then cut a 5mm (¼in) deep square in the top of each. Bake for 10 minutes, reduce the temperature to 190°C (375°F/Gas 5), and bake for a further 25–35 minutes, or until the bases sound hollow when tapped. Transfer to a wire rack and leave to cool.

makes 2 loaves

**prep 20 mins,
plus rising
• cook 35–45 mins**

**freeze for up to
3 months**

Plaited loaf

This enriched fruit loaf makes a lovely teatime treat, and it's also great toasted.

INGREDIENTS

250ml (8fl oz) whipping cream
500g (1lb 2oz) plain flour
7g sachet fast-action dried yeast
85g (3 oz) caster sugar
few drops of pure vanilla extract
zest of 1 lemon

pinch of salt
3 eggs
oil, for greasing
flour, for dusting
200g (7 oz) raisins
2 tsp milk

METHOD

1 To make the dough, gently warm the cream in a small saucepan. Mix together the flour and dried yeast in a large bowl, then add the sugar, vanilla extract, lemon zest, and salt.

2 Separate 1 of the eggs and set aside the yolk. Add the egg white to the flour mixture, along with the remaining 2 eggs and the warmed cream. Using a wooden spoon or mixer with a kneading hook, start mixing gently to combine the ingredients, then mix and knead together for about 5 minutes, or until it forms a smooth dough. Cover with a tea towel and put in a warm place until doubled in size.

3 Grease a large baking tray. Dust the dough with flour and add the raisins. Remove from the bowl and knead briefly on a lightly floured surface until everything is incorporated. Take two-thirds of the dough and make 3 x 40cm (16in) long sausage shapes. Plait them together and put onto the baking tray. Using a rolling pin, make a depression lengthways along the whole plaited bun.

4 Beat together the reserved egg yolk and milk and brush the depression with a little of this mixture. Divide the remaining dough into 3 equal portions, roll into thin sausage shapes about 35cm (14in) long and plait. Place this plait into the depression on the larger plait and brush all over with the egg and milk.

5 Return, uncovered, to a warm place until it has doubled in size. Preheat the oven to 180°C (350°F/Gas 4) for 40 minutes, or until golden brown and well risen. Leave to cool on a wire rack before serving.

makes 1 loaf

prep 35 mins,
plus rising
• cook 40 mins

Brioche

A sweet morning bread that is ideally served warm.

INGREDIENTS

375g (13 oz) strong white flour
50g (1¾ oz) caster sugar
7g sachet fast-action dried yeast
2 tsp salt
100ml (3½fl oz) milk, warmed
4 eggs, 1 beaten for glazing
175g (6 oz) unsalted butter, softened
oil, for greasing

METHOD

1 Mix together the flour, sugar, yeast, and salt, then add the milk and 3 of the eggs. Mix to a dough and knead for 10 minutes. Add the butter and knead for another 10 minutes. Put the dough in a lightly oiled bowl and refrigerate overnight. (To mix using an electric mixer, see step-by-step technique on p7.)

2 Grease the tins. Lightly knead the dough, then divide into 12 pieces. Cut a quarter off 1 piece, and form both pieces into balls. Place the large ball in the tin and the small ball of dough on top, securing it by pressing the floured handle of a wooden spoon through the centre. Repeat with the remaining dough.

3 Cover loosely and leave to rise for 30 minutes. Preheat the oven to 190°C (375°F/Gas 5). Glaze the risen brioche with the beaten egg, making sure it doesn't drip down the sides. Bake for 10–12 minutes, or until golden brown, and cool on a wire rack.

makes 12 brioche

prep 35–45 mins, plus chilling and rising • cook 10–12 mins

chill the dough overnight

12 × 7.5cm (3in) brioche tins

Focaccia

This version of a traditional Italian-style bread is easy to make.

INGREDIENTS

500g (1lb 2oz) strong white flour
7g sachet fast-action yeast
1 tsp salt
4 tbsp olive oil, plus extra for oiling
3 tbsp extra virgin olive oil
½–1 tbsp coarse sea salt

METHOD

1 Tip the flour into a bowl and stir in the yeast and salt. Stir the olive oil into 300ml (10fl oz) tepid water and add to the bowl. Mix to a soft dough, adding more water if necessary. Turn the dough out on to a lightly floured surface and knead for 8–10 minutes, or until it is smooth and elastic. Cover the dough loosely with a piece of oiled cling film and leave it in a warm place for 1½ hours, or until doubled in size.

2 Roll the dough out to a 25 x 40cm (10 x 16in) rectangle. Brush half of the extra virgin olive oil over half of the dough. Brush water around the edges of the other half and fold the dough in half, to give a 25 x 20cm (10 x 8in) rectangle. Place it on the baking tray and press your knuckles down into the dough to give it a dimpled surface. Cover the dough with a tea towel and leave it to rise in a warm place for another 30–40 minutes.

3 Preheat the oven to 200°C (400°F/Gas 6). Drizzle the remaining extra virgin olive oil over the dough, leaving it to pool slightly in the dimpled dough. Sprinkle over the sea salt – or, for a tasty variation, add some rosemary as well. Bake in the centre of the oven for 30–35 minutes, or until it is risen and golden in colour.

4 Remove the baking tray from the oven, slide the bread on to a wire rack, and leave it to cool. Serve the bread on the day of baking, either warm or cold, cut into chunks.

makes 1 loaf

prep 15 mins,
plus rising
• cook 30–35 mins

freeze for up to
2 months

Crusty white loaf

A basic white bread dough that you can use for various shapes of loaf, or rolls.

INGREDIENTS

450g (1lb) strong plain flour, plus extra
  for dusting
1½ tsp fast-action dried yeast
1 tsp salt
1 tsp sugar
1 tbsp vegetable oil, sunflower, or
  light olive oil, plus extra for oiling

METHOD

1. Stir the flour and yeast together in a large bowl, then mix in the salt and sugar. Make a well in the middle and pour in the oil and 300ml (10fl oz) tepid water. Mix to form a soft dough, adding more water if required.

2. Turn out on to a lightly floured work surface and knead the dough for 5–10 minutes, or until smooth and elastic. Shape into a round by tucking all of the edges into the middle, then put into a large oiled bowl, smooth-side up. Cover loosely with oiled cling film and leave in a warm place for 1 hour, or until doubled in size.

3. Oil and flour the inside of the loaf tin, tapping out the excess flour. When the dough has risen, lightly knead the dough and press it into a rough rectangle shape. Tuck the shorter ends in, followed by the longer edges, then lay it, seam-side down, in the loaf tin. Cover loosely with the oiled cling film and leave for 30 minutes, or until risen.

4. Preheat the oven to 220°C (425°F/Gas 7). Dust the top of the loaf with more flour, slash the top with a sharp knife, then bake for 20 minutes. Reduce the oven to 200°C (400°F/Gas 6) and bake for another 20 minutes, or until risen with golden crust. Turn out the loaf and check that it is cooked; it will sound hollow when tapped on the base. Transfer to a wire rack to cool.

makes 1
large loaf

prep 35 mins,
plus rising
• cook 40 mins

900g (2lb)
loaf tin

freeze for up to
1 month

Morning rolls

Easy-to-make soft white rolls that are ideal for breakfast.

INGREDIENTS

500g (1lb 2oz) strong white flour
2 tsp light soft brown sugar
7g sachet fast-action dried yeast
2 tsp salt

METHOD

1 Place the flour, sugar, yeast, and salt into a large bowl. Add 250ml (9fl oz) tepid water, or enough to form a soft, pliable dough. Knead well for 10 minutes. Place in a lightly oiled bowl and loosely cover. Leave in a warm place to rise for 1 hour, or until doubled in size.

2 Turn the dough out on to a lightly floured surface and knead briefly. Divide it into 16 pieces and shape into balls. Smooth the tops and place on to 2 lightly oiled baking trays. Leave enough space for them to spread out without touching. Leave to rise in a warm place for 30 minutes, or until doubled in size.

3 Preheat the oven to 200°C (400°F/Gas 6). Bake the rolls for 20 minutes, or until they are brown on top and sound hollow when tapped on the base.

makes 16

prep 40 mins,
plus rising
• cook 20 mins

freeze for up to
3 months

Sourdough bread with fennel seeds

This bread needs some forward planning, but it is easy to make.

INGREDIENTS

675g (1½lb) strong white flour
7g sachet fast-action dried yeast
1 tbsp caster sugar
1 tsp salt
1 tbsp fennel seeds

For the starter

225g (8 oz) strong white flour
7g sachet fast-action dried yeast

METHOD

1 To make the starter, mix together the flour and dried yeast in a large bowl. Using a wooden spoon, gradually stir in 600ml (1 pint) tepid water to make a smooth batter. Cover with a damp cloth and leave for 2 days, stirring daily and dampening the cloth when necessary to keep it moist.

2 For the bread, mix the flour, yeast, sugar, salt, and fennel seeds together in a large bowl. Make a hollow in the middle. Stir the starter dough, which will have separated, and add 150ml (5fl oz) of the starter and 350ml (12fl oz) tepid water to the dry ingredients.

3 Mix to a soft, pliable dough. Add a further 1–2 tbsp of water if the mixture is too dry. Knead on a lightly floured surface for 10 minutes, or until the dough is smooth and elastic. Shape into a ball and place in an oiled bowl. Cover loosely and leave in a warm place for 1 hour, or until doubled in size.

4 Grease a large baking tray. Remove the dough from the bowl and knead briefly. Shape into a flattish round and place on the baking tray. Cover with a damp cloth and leave to rise for 1 hour, or until doubled in size.

5 Preheat the oven to 220°C (425°F/Gas 7). Lightly dust the loaf with flour, then, using a sharp knife, slash the top in a diamond pattern. Bake for 15 minutes, then reduce the temperature to 190°C (375°F/Gas 5) and bake for a further 20–25 minutes, or until the bread is golden and sounds hollow when tapped on the base. Transfer to a wire rack and leave to cool.

makes 1
large loaf

prep 40 mins, plus
standing and rising
• cook 35–40 mins

make the starter
at least 2 days
in advance

freeze for up to
1 month

Crumpets

Toasted crumpets are great with sweet or savoury toppings.

INGREDIENTS

125g (4½ oz) plain white flour
125g (4½ oz) strong white flour
½ tsp fast-action dried yeast
175ml (6fl oz) tepid milk
½ tsp salt
½ tsp bicarbonate of soda

METHOD

1 Mix together the flours and yeast. Stir in the milk and 175ml (6fl oz) tepid water, and leave for 2 hours, or until the bubbles have risen and then started to fall again. Mix the salt and bicarbonate of soda into 2 tablespoons of lukewarm water and whisk into the batter. Set aside for 5 minutes.

2 Oil 4 crumpet rings. Lightly oil a large, heavy frying pan and place the rings in the pan.

3 Pour the batter into a jug. Heat the pan over a medium heat and pour batter into each ring to a depth of 1–2cm (½–¾in). Cook the crumpets for 8–10 minutes, or until the batter has set all the way through and the top is covered in holes. If no bubbles appear, the mixture is too dry so stir a little water into the remaining batter.

4 Lift the rings off the crumpets, turn them over, and cook for another 2–3 minutes, or until just golden. Repeat with the remaining batter. Serve the freshly cooked crumpets warm and buttered, or toast to reheat if serving them later.

makes 8

prep 10 mins,
plus resting
• cook 20–26 mins

crumpet rings
or 10cm (4in)
metal cutters

freeze for up to
1 month

Wholemeal bread

A blend of white and wholemeal flour makes
a lighter, moister loaf.

INGREDIENTS

225g (8 oz) strong white flour, plus
  extra for kneading
225g (8 oz) strong wholemeal flour,
  plus extra for dusting
1½ tsp fast-action dried yeast
1 tsp salt

1 tbsp vegetable oil, sunflower oil, or
  light olive oil, plus extra for oiling
1 tbsp honey
200ml (7fl oz) lukewarm milk
1 beaten egg, to glaze

METHOD

1 Mix the flours, yeast, and salt in a large bowl, then make a well. Stir the oil, honey,
  milk, and 150ml (5fl oz) lukewarm water in a jug until the honey has dissolved. Pour
  into the well in the centre of the dry ingredients. Mix to form a slightly sticky dough.
  Stand for 10 minutes.

2 Dust the work surface with a little flour, then knead the dough for 5–10 minutes, or
  until it is smooth and springs back when pressed lightly. Shape into a ball and place
  in a large oiled bowl. Cover loosely with oiled cling film and leave in a warm place for
  1 hour, or until doubled in size. Meanwhile, oil and flour the inside of the loaf tin,
  tapping out the excess flour.

3 When risen, turn out on to a lightly floured surface and knead briefly. Press the dough
  into a rough rectangle shape and tuck the shorter ends in, followed by the longer
  edges. Lay it, seam-side down, in the tin, cover loosely with oiled cling film, and leave
  for 30 minutes, or until doubled in size.

4 Preheat the oven to 220°C (425°F/Gas 7). Sieve a little wholemeal flour, leaving the
  bran in the sieve. Brush the egg over the loaf to glaze, scatter the bran over, then slash
  it with a sharp knife. Bake for 20 minutes, then reduce the heat to 200°C (400°F/Gas 6)
  and bake for another 20 minutes, or until risen with a dark golden crust. Tip the loaf
  out of the tin, then let it cool completely on a wire rack.

makes
1 loaf

prep 35 mins, plus
rising • cook 40 mins

900g (2lb)
loaf tin

Ciabatta

This slipper-shaped Italian bread is made using a starter that rises overnight.

INGREDIENTS

450g (1lb) Italian "oo" flour
1½ tsp fast-action dried yeast
2 tsp olive oil, plus extra for brushing
1 tsp salt

For the starter

175g (6 oz) Italian "oo" flour
¼ tsp fast-action dried yeast

METHOD

1 To make the starter, place the flour, yeast, and 100ml (3½fl oz) lukewarm water in a bowl. Mix well for a few minutes until the mixture forms a ball. Place inside a lightly oiled bowl, roll around the bowl to coat in the oil, cover, and leave overnight in a warm place.

2 The next day, make the dough by mixing the flour, yeast, oil, salt, and 350ml (12fl oz) tepid water. Once combined, add the starter and continue kneading until you have a wet, sticky dough.

3 Place the dough in a lightly oiled bowl. Roll it around the bowl to coat in the oil, then leave to rise in a warm place for 2 hours, or until doubled in size.

4 Preheat the oven to 220°C (425°F/Gas 7). Punch the dough back and knead for 10 minutes, or until smooth and elastic. Mould the dough into a slipper shape and place it on an oiled baking tray. Bake for 10 minutes, reduce the temperature to 190°C (375°F/Gas 5), and bake for a further 30 minutes, or until a crust forms and the loaf sounds hollow when tapped underneath. Cool on a wire rack.

makes 1 loaf

prep 30 mins, plus standing and rising • cook 40 mins

make the starter the day before baking

Onion and herb loaf

A delicious savoury loaf with herb-flavoured dough and a fried onion filling.

INGREDIENTS

550g (1¼lb) strong white flour
1 tsp fast-action dried yeast
1 heaped tsp salt
1 tbsp finely chopped rosemary, plus
   2–3 extra sprigs, rubbed in oil
5 tbsp extra virgin olive oil
1 egg, beaten

For the filling

2 tbsp olive oil
½ tsp salt
½ tsp coarsely crushed black pepper
2 onions, sliced
1 tbsp balsamic vinegar
3 tbsp golden caster sugar
1 tbsp rosemary or thyme, finely chopped

METHOD

1 Place 225g (8 oz) of the flour in a bowl, add 300ml (10fl oz) tepid water and the yeast, mix well, and leave for 1 hour. Add the remaining flour, salt, rosemary, and oil, and mix to a soft, pliable dough. Knead on a lightly floured surface for 10 minutes, or until elastic.

2 Shape the dough into a ball and place in a large oiled bowl. Cover loosely with oiled cling film, and leave in a warm place for 1 hour, or until doubled in size.

3 For the filling, heat the oil in a frying pan, add the salt and black pepper, then add the onions and fry on a medium heat for 10 minutes, or until golden. Stir in the remaining ingredients and fry for 2–4 minutes, or until dark and sticky.

4 Turn the dough out on to a floured surface and knead briefly. Press into a large rectangle shape, then spread with the filling. Fold the shorter sides in, then fold the bottom third up, and the top third down, like an envelope. Press gently then turn over and lift on to a lightly floured baking tray, and shape the ends of the loaf into slight points. Cover loosely and leave for 30 minutes, or until doubled in size. Preheat the oven to 220°C (425°F/Gas 7).

5 Brush the dough with beaten egg, sprinkle with flour, then slash it with a sharp knife to reveal the filling inside. Sprinkle with the rosemary rubbed in oil, then bake for 20 minutes. Reduce the oven to 200°C (400°F/Gas 6) and bake for 20 minutes, or until the bread is risen and a deep golden brown.

makes 1 loaf

**prep 35 mins, plus
rising • cook 55 mins**

English muffins

A soft traditional English bread that is great for brunch.

INGREDIENTS

450g (1lb) strong white flour
1 tsp fast-action dried yeast
1 tsp salt
25g (scant 1 oz) butter, melted
25g (scant 1 oz) ground rice or semolina

METHOD

1 Mix the flour, yeast, and salt in a large bowl. Add the melted butter and 300ml (10fl oz) tepid water and mix to a soft, pliable dough.
2 Knead the dough for 5 minutes. Shape into a ball and place in a large oiled bowl. Cover loosely with oiled cling film and leave in a warm place for 1 hour, or until doubled in size. Lay a tea towel on a tray and scatter with most of the ground rice.
3 Turn out the dough, knead briefly, and divide into 10 balls. Place on the tea towel and press into flattish rounds. Sprinkle with the rest of the ground rice and cover with another tea towel. Leave for 20–30 minutes, or until risen.
4 Heat a large lidded frying pan and cook the muffins in batches. Cover with the lid and cook very gently for 10–12 minutes, or until they puff up and the undersides are golden and toasted. Turn over and cook for 3–4 minutes, or until golden underneath. Cool on a wire rack.

makes 10

prep 25–30 mins, plus
rising • cook 13–16 mins

Spiced fruit buns

These delicious sweetened rolls make a perfect afternoon snack.

INGREDIENTS

500g (1lb 2oz) strong white bread flour
7g sachet fast-action dried yeast
1 tsp mixed spice
½ tsp ground nutmeg
1 tsp salt
6 tbsp caster sugar

60g (2 oz) butter
240ml (8fl oz) tepid milk
150g (5½ oz) mixed dried fruit
2 tbsp icing sugar
¼ tsp pure vanilla extract

METHOD

1 Place the flour, yeast, spices, salt, and caster sugar in a large mixing bowl. Rub in the butter. Add enough milk to form a soft, pliable dough. Knead well for 10 minutes. Shape into a ball, then place in a lightly oiled bowl and cover loosely. Leave in a warm place to rise for 1 hour.

2 Tip the dough on to a lightly floured work surface and knead gently. Knead in the dried fruit. Divide the dough into 12 pieces, roll into balls, and place, well spaced, on lightly greased baking trays. Cover loosely and place in a warm place for 30 minutes, or until doubled in size.

3 Preheat the oven to 200°C (400°F/Gas 6). Bake for 15 minutes, or until the buns sound hollow when tapped on the bottom. Transfer to a wire rack to cool. While the buns are still hot, combine the icing sugar, vanilla extract, and 1 tbsp cold water, and brush over the top of the buns to glaze.

makes 12

prep 30 mins, plus
rising • cook 15 mins

Rye bread

Breads made with rye flour are very popular in central and eastern Europe.

INGREDIENTS

150g (5½ oz) rye flour
200g (7 oz) strong white flour, plus extra for dusting
2 tsp salt
1 egg, beaten
1 tsp caraway seeds, to decorate

For the starter

150g (5½ oz) rye flour
150g (5½ oz) pot live natural yogurt
1 tsp fast-action dried yeast
1 tbsp black treacle
1 tsp caraway seeds, lightly crushed

METHOD

1 Mix all of the starter ingredients together with 250ml (9fl oz) tepid water. Cover and leave overnight, until bubbling.

2 The next day, mix the flours together with the salt, then stir into the starter. Mix to make a dough, adding a little extra water if required.

3 Turn out on to a lightly floured surface and knead the dough for 5–10 minutes, or until smooth and springy. Shape into a ball, put into an oiled bowl and cover loosely with oiled cling film. Leave in a warm place for 1 hour, or until doubled in size.

4 Flour a baking tray. Lightly knead the dough again, then form it into a rugby-ball shape. Lift on to the tray, re-cover it loosely, and leave to rise again for another 30 minutes. Preheat the oven to 220°C (425°F/Gas 7).

5 Brush the dough with the egg, sprinkle with the caraway seeds, and slash the loaf along its length with a sharp knife. Bake for 20 minutes, then reduce the heat to 200°C (400°F/Gas 6) and bake for another 20–30 minutes, or until dark golden with a hard shiny crust. Cool on a wire rack.

makes 1 large loaf

prep 25 mins, plus rising • cook 40–50 mins

make the starter the day before baking

Croissants

These may take time to make but the final result is well worth the effort.

INGREDIENTS

300g (10 oz) strong white flour
1 tsp salt
30g (1 oz) sugar

7g sachet fast-action dried yeast
250g (9 oz) butter, chilled
1 egg, beaten

METHOD

1 Place the flour, salt, sugar, and yeast in a large bowl. Using a table knife, slowly mix in enough water to form a soft dough. Knead on a lightly floured surface until the dough becomes more elastic. Place back in the bowl, cover with lightly oiled cling film, and chill for 1 hour.

2 Roll out a rectangle that measures 30 x 15cm (12 x 6in). Squash the butter, patting down the shape, until it is 1cm (½in) thick. The butter will make a smaller rectangle than the dough. If the butter has become too warm, chill it briefly. Place the butter in the centre of the dough. Fold the dough over so the butter is encased, and chill for 1 hour.

3 Roll out the dough on a lightly floured surface to a 30 x 15cm (12 x 6in) rectangle. Fold the right third over to the centre, then fold the left third over the top so you have 3 layers to your dough. Chill for 1 hour, until firm.

4 Repeat the folding and chilling process twice more, then wrap in cling film and chill overnight.

5 The next day, roll out the dough on a lightly floured surface to a 3mm (1/8in) thick square. Cut into 10 x 10cm (4 x 4in) squares, then cut diagonally to make triangles of dough. Holding the points at either end of the longer lengths, roll the dough towards you, pulling the points gently. The end points should not fold underneath the croissants; if they do, reshape them, rolling more loosely. Place on oiled baking trays, leaving plenty of space between each, and curve them into crescent shapes. Cover with lightly oiled cling film and leave for 1 hour, or until doubled in size but keeping their shape.

6 Preheat the oven to 240°C (475°F/Gas 9). Brush the croissants with the beaten egg and bake for 10 minutes, then reduce the oven temperature to 190°C (375°F/Gas 5) and bake for 10–15 minutes, or until golden brown. Cool on a wire rack.

makes 10

prep 1 hr, plus chilling and rising • cook 20–25 mins

allow at least 5 hrs to prepare before chilling overnight

Chapatis

In India, these unleavened breads are cooked in a concave pan called a *tava* but a cast-iron frying pan works well.

INGREDIENTS

250g (9 oz) chapati flour or
   wholemeal plain flour, plus
   extra for dusting
1 tsp salt
ghee or melted butter,
   for brushing

METHOD

1 Sift the flour into a bowl and discard any bran left in the sieve. Make a well in the centre, add 40ml (3 tbsp) cold water and mix together. Work in the salt, then add another 60ml (2fl oz) cold water and mix until the dough starts to come together.

2 Gradually add another 60ml (2fl oz) cold water to make a sticky dough. Keep kneading the dough in the bowl until it is firm, elastic, and less sticky.

3 Cover with a tea towel and leave to rest for 15 minutes, or until the dough becomes firmer, and no longer sticky.

4 Dust your hands with flour and pull off egg-sized pieces of dough. Shape into balls, then roll out into rounds 18cm (7in) in diameter.

5 Heat the ungreased frying pan and cook the chapatis for 30 seconds on each side, or until golden and speckled. Remove from the pan and brush with ghee or melted butter, keeping them warm as you cook the rest.

makes 8

prep 30 mins,
plus resting
• cook 10 mins

tava or heavy
cast-iron
frying pan

Pitta bread

These Middle Eastern flat breads are essential for serving with salads and dips.

INGREDIENTS

500g (1lb 2oz) strong white bread flour,
  plus extra for dusting
1 tsp fast-action dried yeast
1 tsp caster sugar
1 tsp salt
4 tbsp olive oil, plus extra for greasing

METHOD

1 Mix together the first 4 ingredients in a large bowl. Make a well in the centre and add 4 tablespoons of olive oil and 300ml (10fl oz) lukewarm water. Using a wooden spoon, start mixing gently to combine the ingredients and then mix and knead together for 5 minutes, or until it forms a smooth dough. Cover with a tea towel and put the dough in a warm place for 1 hour, or until it has doubled in size.

2 Dust the work surface with flour and knead the dough briefly until smooth. Divide into 8 equal pieces and roll each out into a thin oval shape, about 20cm (8in) long. Grease 2 large baking trays and place 4 dough ovals on each. Cover with oiled cling film and leave in a warm place for 20 minutes, or until the dough is slightly risen.

3 Preheat the oven to 220°C (425°F/Gas 7). Brush the tops with a little olive oil and bake for 10 minutes, or until puffed and golden brown. Carefully transfer to a wire rack and serve while still warm.

makes 8

prep 20 mins,
plus resting •
cook 10 mins

freeze, cooled and
wrapped, for up
to 3 months

Naan bread

This familiar Indian flat bread is traditionally cooked in a tandoor oven but this recipe uses a conventional oven.

INGREDIENTS

500g (1lb 2oz) strong white bread flour,
  plus extra for dusting
1¼ tsp fast-action dried yeast
1 tsp caster sugar
1½ tsp salt
2 tsp black onion seeds
100ml (3½fl oz) full-fat plain yogurt
50g (2 oz) ghee or butter, melted

METHOD

1 Mix together the flour and the yeast in a large bowl, then add the sugar, salt, and onion seeds.

2 Make a well in the centre of the dry ingredients and add 200ml (7fl oz) lukewarm water, the yogurt, and the melted ghee. Using a wooden spoon, start mixing gently to combine the ingredients for 5 minutes, or until it forms a smooth dough. Cover with a tea towel and put it in a warm place for 1 hour, or until it has doubled in size.

3 Preheat the oven to its hottest setting and place 2 large baking trays in the oven. Dust the work surface with flour and knead the dough briefly until smooth. Divide into 4 equal pieces and roll each piece into an oval shape about 25cm (10in) long.

4 Carefully transfer the breads on to the preheated baking trays and cook in the oven for 6–7 minutes, or until well puffed.

5 Meanwhile, preheat the grill to its hottest setting. Transfer the breads to the grill pan and cook them for 30–40 seconds on each side, or until they brown and blister; take care not to put the breads too close to the heat source, otherwise they may catch and burn. Carefully transfer to a wire rack and serve while still warm.

makes 4

prep 20 mins, plus resting • cook 9 mins

freeze, cooled and wrapped, for up to 3 months

Moroccan spiced flatbreads

Best eaten on the day they are made, these breads are good as they are, or lightly chargrilled.

INGREDIENTS

1½ tsp cumin seeds, plus more to decorate

1½ tsp ground coriander

450g (1lb) strong white flour, plus extra for kneading

1 tsp fast-action dried yeast

1 tsp salt

1 small bunch of coriander, roughly chopped

200g can chickpeas, drained and roughly crushed

150g (5½oz) plain yogurt

1 tbsp olive oil, plus extra for brushing

METHOD

1 Toast the cumin and ground coriander in a dry pan for 1 minute until fragrant. Mix the flour, yeast, and salt in a large bowl. Stir in the spices, coriander, and chickpeas, then make a well in the middle. Pour in the yogurt, oil, and 300ml (10fl oz) warm water, and bring together quickly to form a sticky dough. Set aside in the bowl for 10 minutes.

2 Turn the dough out on to a lightly floured surface. Knead for 5 minutes. Shape into a ball and place in a large oiled bowl. Cover loosely with oiled cling film and leave for 1 hour in a warm place, or until doubled in size.

3 Lightly dust 2 large baking trays with flour. Preheat the oven to 220°C (425°F/Gas 7). Turn the dough out on to a floured surface and cut into 8 even-sized pieces. Using a rolling pin, flatten out into ovals about 5mm (¼in) thick. Place on the baking trays, brush with a little oil, and scatter with a few cumin seeds. Bake for 15 minutes, or until the breads are golden and puffed up. Serve with bowls of hummus or tapenade, lamb koftas, and salads.

makes 8

prep 25 mins, plus resting • cook 15 mins

Scotch pancakes

These thick, little pancakes are also called drop scones because the batter is dropped onto a frying pan.

INGREDIENTS
225g (8 oz) plain white flour
4 tsp baking powder
1 large egg
2 tsp golden syrup
200ml (7fl oz) milk
vegetable oil, for frying

METHOD
1 Place the frying pan over a medium heat. Fold a tea towel in half and lay it on a baking tray.
2 Sift the flour and baking powder into a bowl; make a well in the centre and add the egg, golden syrup, and milk. Whisk well to make a smooth batter the consistency of thick cream. If the mixture is too thick, beat in a little more milk.
3 Test that the frying pan is hot enough by sprinkling a little flour on to the hot surface; it should slowly brown. If it burns, the pan is too hot and needs to cool a little. When the temperature is right, carefully dust off the flour and rub a piece of kitchen towel dipped in cooking oil lightly over the surface. Use oven gloves to protect your hands.
4 Lift out 1 tablespoon of batter, cleaning the back of the spoon on the edge of the bowl. Drop the batter from the tip of the spoon on to the hot pan to make a nice round shape. Repeat, leaving enough room between the rounds for the pancakes to rise and spread.
5 Bubbles will appear on the surface of the pancakes. When they begin to burst, ease a palette knife underneath the pancakes and gently flip to cook the other side. To ensure even browning, lightly press the flat blade on the cooked side after you have turned the pancake; place cooked pancakes inside the folded towel to keep them soft while you fry the rest of the batch.
6 Oil the hot pan after each batch and watch the heat. If the pancakes are pale and take a long time to cook, turn up the heat. If they brown too quickly on the outside and are still raw in the middle, reduce the heat. They are best eaten freshly baked and warm.

makes 12   **prep 10 mins**   **freeze for up to**
                      • cook 15 mins   **1 month**

Waffles

These easy-to-make waffles are perfect for breakfast,
a light snack, or dessert.

INGREDIENTS

175g (6 oz) plain flour
1 tsp baking powder
2 tbsp caster sugar
300ml (10fl oz) milk
75g (2½ oz) butter, melted
1 tsp pure vanilla extract
2 large eggs, separated

METHOD

1 Place the flour, baking powder, and caster sugar in a food processor and process to
   mix. In a jug, combine the milk, melted butter, vanilla extract, and egg yolks. Pour in
   and process until just blended. If you do not have a food processor, place the dry
   ingredients in a bowl, make a well in the centre, and pour in the wet ingredients.
   Gradually whisk in the flour.
2 Preheat the waffle maker or iron. In a clean large bowl whisk the egg white until it
   stands in soft peaks. Add to the processor or blender, and pulse for 1–2 seconds, or
   until just combined. Alternatively, fold into the batter with a metal spoon. Do not
   over-process or you will lose all the air and the waffles will be tough.
3 Preheat the oven to 130°C (250°F/Gas ½). Spoon a small ladleful of the batter on to the
   hot iron (or the amount recommended by the waffle maker manufacturer) and spread
   almost to the edge. Close the lid and bake until golden. Serve immediately, or keep
   warm in a single layer in the oven.

makes 6–8

prep 10 mins
• cook 20–25 mins

waffle maker or
waffle iron

freeze for up
to 1 month

Scones

There is nothing better for afternoon tea than freshly baked crumbly scones.

INGREDIENTS

225g (8 oz) self-raising flour, plus extra
  for dusting
½ tsp salt
50g (1¾ oz) sultanas
60g (2 oz) butter, cubed
30g (1 oz) sugar
150ml (5fl oz) milk
1 egg, beaten

METHOD

1 Preheat the oven to 220°C (425°F/Gas 7). Sift the flour and the salt into a large mixing bowl, then add the sultanas and mix together. Rub in the butter with your fingertips, until the mixture resembles coarse breadcrumbs, then mix in the sugar. Make a well in the centre and pour in the milk, then stir together, bringing in the flour from the edges, with a knife or spoon.
2 Turn the soft, sticky dough on to a lightly floured work surface. Knead until smooth, then shape into a 2.5cm (1in) thick circle.
3 Dip the cutter in flour, then use to cut rounds from the dough. Re-form the dough, if necessary, to cut sufficient scones.
4 Place the scones on a baking tray and brush the tops with a little beaten egg. Put the tray on to the top shelf of the oven and bake for 12–15 minutes, or until golden. Remove from the oven and cool on a wire rack. Serve while still warm.

makes 8

prep 25 mins
• cook 12–15 mins

6cm (2½in) round
pastry cutter

Mini chocolate nut pastries

Tasty bite-sized chocolate pastries – the perfect treat.

INGREDIENTS

115g (4 oz) ground hazelnuts
1½ tbsp icing sugar, plus extra
  for dusting
3 tbsp amaretto or almond-flavoured
  liqueur
75g (2½ oz) dark chocolate, grated
4 x filo pastry sheets, 18 x 30cm
  (7 x 12in)
3 tbsp clear honey, warmed

METHOD

1 Preheat the oven to 190°C (375°F/Gas 5). Lightly grease a baking tray. Mix the hazelnuts, icing sugar, amaretto, and chocolate until combined.
2 Cut out 24 squares, each 10cm (4in), from the filo. Place some filling in the middle of each square. Brush a little water around the edge, gather the sides around the filling, and pinch into a purse-like shape.
3 Place the pastries on the baking tray and bake for 10–12 minutes, or until golden. Brush gently with honey, leave for 5 minutes, then dust with icing sugar. Serve warm or cold.

makes 24

prep 25 mins
• cook 10–12 mins

Mini chocolate éclairs

These French choux pastries are perfect for
a teatime indulgence.

INGREDIENTS

75g (2½ oz) butter
125g (4½ oz) plain flour
3 eggs
500ml (16fl oz) double cream
   or whipping cream
200g (7 oz) dark chocolate

METHOD

1 Preheat the oven to 200°C (400°F/Gas 6). Melt the butter in a pan with 200ml (7fl oz)
   cold water, then bring to the boil, remove from the heat, and stir in the flour. Beat with
   a wooden spoon until well combined.
2 Lightly beat the eggs and add to the flour and butter mixture a little at a time, whisking
   constantly. Continue whisking until the mixture is smooth and glossy and comes away
   easily from the sides of the pan. Spoon it into a piping bag.
3 Pipe 5cm (2in) lengths of the mixture on to 2 baking trays lined with baking parchment.
   You should have around 30 in all. Bake for 20 minutes or until golden brown, then
   remove from the oven and make a slit down the side of each one. Return to the oven
   for 5 minutes for the insides to cook through, then remove and leave to cool.
4 Put the cream in a mixing bowl and whisk until soft peaks form. Spoon or pipe the
   cream into each éclair. Break the chocolate into pieces and place in a heatproof bowl.
   Sit the bowl over a pan of simmering water and stir until the chocolate is melted and
   smooth. Spoon over the éclairs and serve.

makes 30

**prep 30 mins
• cook 30 mins**

**electric hand
whisk; piping bag**

Silesian poppy tart

Tarts made with poppy seeds are popular in Eastern Europe.

INGREDIENTS

1 litre (1¾ pints) milk
150g (5½ oz) butter
200g (7 oz) semolina
200g (7 oz) poppy seeds
175g (6 oz) caster sugar
1 tsp pure vanilla extract
2 eggs
100g (3½ oz) curd cheese
50g (1¾ oz) ground almonds
50g (1¾ oz) raisins
1 pear, peeled, cored, and grated
icing sugar, for dusting

For the pastry

250g (9 oz) plain flour
2 tsp baking powder
125g (4½ oz) caster sugar
2–3 drops pure vanilla extract
pinch of salt
1 egg
125g (4½ oz) butter, softened

METHOD

1 To make the pastry, sift the flour with the baking powder into a bowl. Add the sugar, vanilla, salt, egg, butter, and a little water. Mix to make a dough, roll into a ball using your hands, and set aside.

2 Place the milk and butter in a saucepan and bring to the boil. Gradually stir in the semolina and poppy seeds. Simmer over a low heat for 20 minutes, stirring occasionally, then remove from the heat and allow to cool for 10 minutes.

3 Preheat the oven to 180°C (350°F/Gas 4) and grease the base of the tin. Roll out half of the dough and fit it into the base. Roll out the remaining dough into a long strip, and press it to the side of the tin to form an edge 3cm (1¼in) high.

4 Stir together the sugar, vanilla, eggs, curd cheese, almonds, and raisins into the cooled poppy seed and semolina mixture. Stir in the pear, pour the mixture evenly into the pastry base, and bake for 1 hour.

5 Place the tin on to a wire rack to cool, loosen the edge of the tart with a knife, and remove the ring. Dust with icing sugar before serving.

serves 8

prep 35 mins, plus cooling • cook 1 hr 30 mins

28cm (11in) springform tin

Pecan pie

This sweet, crunchy pie originated in the southern United States, where pecan nuts are widely grown.

INGREDIENTS

375g packet ready-made sweet
  dessert pastry
flour, for dusting
150ml (5fl oz) maple syrup
60g (2 oz) butter
175g (6 oz) light soft brown sugar
few drops of pure vanilla extract
pinch of salt
3 eggs
200g (7 oz) pecan nuts

METHOD

1 Roll the pastry out on a lightly floured surface, then use it to line the flan tin. Trim around the top edge of the tin, and prick the base all over with a fork. Chill for at least 30 minutes.

2 Preheat the oven to 200°C (400°F/Gas 6). Line the pastry case with greaseproof paper, and fill with baking beans. Bake for 10 minutes, then remove the paper and beans, and bake for another 10 minutes, or until pale golden. (See technique on p9.) Remove the pastry case from the oven and reduce the temperature to 180°C (350°F/Gas 4).

3 Pour the maple syrup into a saucepan, and add the butter, sugar, vanilla extract, and salt. Place the pan over a low heat, and stir constantly until the butter has melted, and the sugar dissolved. Remove the pan from the heat, and leave the mixture to cool until it feels just tepid, then beat in the eggs, one at a time. Stir in the pecan nuts, then pour the mixture into the pastry case.

4 Bake for 40–50 minutes, or until just set. Cover with a sheet of foil if it is browning too quickly.

5 Remove the pie from the oven, transfer it to a wire rack and leave to cool for 15–20 minutes. Remove from the tin and either serve it warm or leave it on the wire rack to cool completely. Serve with crème fraîche or whipped cream.

serves 8

prep 15 mins,
plus chilling
and cooling
• cook 60–70
mins

23cm (9in)
loose-bottomed
flan tin
• baking beans

Blueberry cream cheese tart

Juicy blueberries perfectly complement the creamy filling.

INGREDIENTS

115g (4 oz) cream cheese
60g (2 oz) soured cream
60g (2 oz) caster sugar
pinch of grated nutmeg
3 eggs, beaten
zest of 1 lemon
350g (12 oz) blueberries
icing sugar, to serve

For the pastry

175g (6 oz) plain flour
85g (3 oz) butter, diced
2 tbsp caster sugar
1 egg yolk

METHOD

1 Place the flour, butter, and sugar in a food processor, and pulse until it resembles breadcrumbs. Or, rub the butter into the flour with your fingertips until it resembles breadcrumbs, then stir in the sugar.

2 Add the egg yolk and mix to a firm dough. Roll out the pastry on a lightly floured surface and use to line the flan tin. Prick the base with a fork. Chill for at least 30 minutes. Preheat the oven to 200°C (400°F/Gas 6).

3 Line the pastry case with greaseproof paper and fill with baking beans. Bake for 10 minutes, then remove the paper and beans and bake for another 10 minutes, or until pale golden. Remove from the oven and reduce the temperature to 180°C (350°F/Gas 4).

4 Beat together the cream cheese, soured cream, sugar, nutmeg, eggs, and lemon zest until well combined. Pour into the pastry case and scatter the blueberries over the surface. Bake for 25–30 minutes, or until just set. Allow to cool before transferring to a serving plate. Serve warm or cold, dusted with icing sugar.

serves 8

prep 25 mins, plus chilling • cook 45–60 mins

23cm (9in) loose-bottomed flan tin • baking beans

Banana cream pie

This traditional American single-crust pie makes
a rich and creamy end to any meal.

INGREDIENTS

500g packet ready-made
  shortcrust pastry
4 large egg yolks
85g (3 oz) caster sugar
4 tbsp cornflour
¼ tsp salt
450ml (15fl oz) full-fat milk

1 tsp pure vanilla extract
3 ripe bananas
½ tbsp lemon juice
350ml (12fl oz) whipping
  cream or double cream
3 tbsp icing sugar

METHOD

1 Preheat the oven to 200°C (400°F/Gas 6). Roll out the pastry on a lightly floured surface to a 30cm (12in) circle, use to line the pie plate and trim off the excess (see p10). Prick the base all over with a fork.

2 Line the pastry with greaseproof paper, fill with baking beans, and place the plate on a baking tray. Bake for 15 minutes, or until the pastry looks pale golden. Lift off the paper and beans and prick the base again. Return to the oven and bake for a further 5–10 minutes, or until the pastry is golden and dry. Transfer the pie plate to a wire rack and leave to cool completely.

3 Meanwhile, beat the egg yolks, sugar, cornflour, and salt until the sugar dissolves and the mixture is pale yellow. Beat in the milk and vanilla. Transfer the mixture to a saucepan over a medium-high heat and bring to just below the boil, stirring until a smooth, thick custard forms. Reduce the heat and stir for 2 minutes. Strain through a fine sieve into a bowl and leave to cool.

4 Thinly slice the bananas and toss with the lemon juice. Spread them out in the pie case, then top with the custard. Cover the pie with cling film and chill for at least 2 hours.

5 Beat the cream until soft peaks form, then sift over the icing sugar, and continue beating until stiff. Spoon the cream over the custard just before serving.

serves 8

prep 20 mins, plus
cooling and chilling
• cook 20–25 mins

allow at least
2 hrs for chilling

23cm (9in) deep pie
plate with a flat rim
• baking beans

Apple pie

A perennial favourite; this convenient version uses ready-made pastry.

INGREDIENTS

375g (13 oz) ready-made shortcrust
  pastry
finely grated zest of 1 lemon
2 tbsp fresh lemon juice
100g (3½oz) caster sugar
4 tbsp plain flour
1 tsp ground mixed spice
7 apples, peeled and thinly sliced
2 tbsp milk, to glaze

METHOD

1 Divide the dough into 2 pieces: one piece should be two-thirds of the dough, the other about one-third. On a lightly floured work surface, roll the larger piece into a 30cm (12in) circle and use to line the pie plate, leaving any excess overhanging. Cover with cling film and chill for at least 15 minutes. Roll out the remaining dough into a 25cm (10in) circle, place on a plate, cover, and refrigerate.

2 Meanwhile, preheat the oven to 200°C (400°F/Gas 6) with a baking tray inside. Mix the lemon zest and juice, sugar, flour, and mixed spice in a large bowl. Gently toss with the apple slices.

3 Tip the filling into the pie plate. Lightly brush the pastry on the rim of the pie plate with water and place the smaller dough circle on top. Crimp the edges together and cut off the excess pastry. Carefully brush the top of the pastry with milk and cut a few slits to allow steam to escape.

4 Put the pie on the hot baking tray in the oven. Reduce the temperature to 190°C (375°F/Gas 5) and bake for 50–55 minutes, or until the pastry is golden brown. Leave to stand for 5 minutes, then slice and serve hot with a scoop of vanilla ice cream or crème Anglaise.

serves 8

prep 25 mins,
plus chilling
• cook
50–55 mins

23cm (9in) deep pie
plate with a flat rim
and a large bowl

Key lime pie

This pie is named for the small limes that grow in the Florida Keys.

INGREDIENTS

100g (3½ oz) butter
225g (8 oz) digestive biscuits, crushed

For the filling

5 limes, plus 1 extra, cut into thin
    slices, to decorate
3 large egg yolks
400g can condensed milk

METHOD

1 Preheat the oven to 180°C (350°F/Gas 4). Melt the butter in a saucepan over a low heat. Add the digestive biscuit crumbs and stir until well combined. Remove from the heat and tip the mixture into the flan tin, then use the base of a metal spoon to press it evenly and firmly all over the base and sides of the tin. Place on a baking tray and bake for 5–10 minutes.

2 Meanwhile, grate the zest of 3 of the limes into a bowl. Juice all 5 of the limes, and set aside.

3 Place the egg yolks into the bowl with the lime zest, and whisk until the egg has thickened. Pour in the condensed milk and continue whisking for 5 minutes if using an electric whisk, or for 6–7 minutes if whisking by hand. Add the lime juice, and whisk again until it is incorporated. Pour the mixture into the tin and bake for 15–20 minutes, or until it is set.

4 Remove the pie from the oven and leave it to cool completely. Serve the pie decorated with the lime slices.

serves 8

prep 20–25 mins plus
cooling • cook 15–20 mins

23cm (9in) loose-
bottomed flan tin

Lemon tart

Variations of this ever-popular tart often appear on restaurant menus.

INGREDIENTS

5 eggs
200g (7 oz) caster sugar
zest and juice of 4 lemons
250ml (9fl oz) double cream
icing sugar, to serve
lemon zest, to serve

For the pastry

175g (6 oz) plain flour, plus
  extra for dusting
85g (3 oz) butter, chilled
45g (1½ oz) caster sugar
1 egg

METHOD

1 To make the pastry, place the flour, butter, and sugar into a food processor and pulse until it resembles breadcrumbs. Add the egg and process until the pastry draws together into a ball.

2 Roll out the pastry on a lightly floured surface into a large circle to line the tart tin. Chill for at least 30 minutes.

3 Beat the eggs and sugar together until combined. Beat in the lemon zest and juice, then whisk in the cream. Chill for 1 hour.

4 Preheat the oven to 190°C (375°F/Gas 5). Line the pastry case with greaseproof paper, fill with baking beans, and bake blind for 10 minutes. Remove the paper and beans, and bake for 5 minutes, or until the base is crisp.

5 Reduce the oven to 140°C (275°F/Gas 1). Place the tart tin on a baking tray. Pour in the lemon filling, being careful not to allow the filling to spill over the edges. Bake for 30 minutes, or until just set. Remove from the oven and cool. Serve, dusted with icing sugar and sprinkled with lemon zest over the top.

serves 8

prep 35 mins, plus chilling and cooling • cook 45 mins

food processor • 24cm (9in) loose-bottomed tart tin • baking beans

Lemon meringue pie

INGREDIENTS

400g (14 oz) ready-made
  shortcrust pastry
6 eggs, separated
3 tbsp cornflour
3 tbsp plain flour
400g (14 oz) caster sugar

juice of 3 lemons
1 tbsp grated lemon zest
45g (1½ oz) butter, diced
½ tsp cream of tartar
½ tsp pure vanilla extract

METHOD

1 Preheat the oven to 200°C (400°F/Gas 6). Lightly grease the flan tin. Roll out the pastry on a lightly floured surface and use to line the tin.

2 Line the pastry case with greaseproof paper, then fill with baking beans. Place on a baking tray and bake for 10–15 minutes, or until the pastry looks pale golden. Lift off the paper and beans, return to the oven, and bake for 3–5 minutes, or until the pastry is golden and dry. Transfer to a wire rack and leave to cool completely. Reduce the heat to 180°C (350°F/Gas 4).

3 Place the egg yolks in a bowl and lightly beat. Combine the cornflour, flour, and 225g (8 oz) of the sugar in a pan. Slowly add 350ml (12fl oz) water and heat gently, stirring, until the sugar dissolves and there are no lumps. Increase the heat slightly and cook, stirring, for 3–5 minutes, or until the mixture starts to thicken.

4 Beat several spoonfuls of the hot mixture into the egg yolks. Pour this mixture into the pan and slowly bring to the boil, stirring constantly. Boil for 3 minutes, then stir in the lemon juice, zest, and butter. Continue boiling for a further 2 minutes, or until the mixture is thick and glossy, stirring constantly and scraping down the side of the pan as necessary. Remove the pan from the heat; cover to keep warm.

5 Whisk the egg whites in a large bowl until foamy. Sprinkle over the cream of tartar and whisk. Continue whisking, adding the remaining sugar, 1 tablespoon at a time. Add the vanilla extract with the last tablespoon of the sugar, whisking until the meringue is thick and glossy.

6 Pour the lemon filling into the pie case, then top with the meringue, spreading it so it completely covers the filling right up to the pastry edge. Take care not to spill it over the pastry or the tart will be difficult to remove from the tin after baking.

7 Place the pie on a baking tray, place in the oven, and bake for 12–15 minutes, or until the meringue is lightly golden. Place the pie on a wire rack and leave to cool completely before serving.

 serves 8

 **prep 30 mins, plus cooling • cook 40–50 mins**

 **23cm (9in) loose-bottomed flan tin • baking beans**

Cannoli

Indulge in crisp Sicilian pastries filled with glacé fruits and ricotta cheese.

INGREDIENTS

175g (6 oz) plain flour, plus extra
   for rolling and dusting
pinch of salt
60g (2 oz) butter
45g (1½ oz) caster sugar
1 egg, beaten
2–3 tbsp dry white wine or Marsala
1 egg white, lightly beaten
oil, for deep-frying

For the filling

60g (2 oz) dark chocolate,
   grated or very finely chopped
350g (12 oz) ricotta cheese
60g (2 oz) icing sugar, plus
   extra to dust
finely grated zest of 1 orange
60g (2 oz) chopped glacé fruits
   or candied citrus peel

METHOD

1 To make the pastry, sift the flour and salt into a bowl, and rub in the butter. Stir in the sugar, mix in the beaten egg, and add enough wine to make a soft dough. Knead until smooth.

2 Roll out the pastry thinly and cut into 16 squares, each measuring roughly 7.5cm (3in). Dust 4 cannoli moulds with flour and wrap a pastry square loosely around each on the diagonal, dampening the edges with lightly beaten egg white and pressing them together to seal.

3 Heat the oil for deep-frying to 180°C (350°F) and deep-fry for 3–4 minutes, or until the pastry is golden and crisp. Drain on a plate lined with kitchen paper, and, when cool enough to handle, carefully twist the metal tubes so you can pull them out of the pastry. Cook 3 more batches in the same way.

4 To make the filling, mix together all the ingredients. When the pastry tubes are cold, pipe or spoon the filling into them. Dust with icing sugar to serve.

makes 16

prep 30 mins, plus cooling • cook 20 mins

deep-fat fryer or large saucepan half filled with oil • cannoli moulds

freeze the uncooked pastry for up to 3 months

Profiteroles

These filled choux pastry buns, drizzled with chocolate sauce, are a deliciously decadent dessert.

INGREDIENTS

60g (2 oz) plain flour
50g (1¾ oz) butter
2 eggs, beaten

For the filling and topping

400ml (14fl oz) double cream
200g (7 oz) dark chocolate,
  broken into pieces
25g (scant 1 oz) butter
2 tbsp golden syrup

METHOD

1 Preheat the oven to 220°C (425°F/ Gas 7). Line 2 large baking trays with greaseproof paper. Sift the flour on to a separate piece of greaseproof paper.

2 Put the butter and 150ml (5fl oz) water into a small saucepan and heat gently until melted. Bring to the boil, remove from the heat, and tip in the flour. Beat quickly with a wooden spoon until the mixture is thick, smooth, and forms a ball in the centre of the saucepan. Cool for 10 minutes.

3 Gradually add the eggs, beating well after each addition. Use enough egg to form a stiff, smooth, and shiny paste. Spoon the mixture into a piping bag fitted with a 1cm (½in) plain nozzle.

4 Pipe walnut-sized rounds, set well apart, on the prepared baking trays. Bake for 20 minutes, or until risen, golden, and crisp. Remove from the oven and make a small slit in the side of each bun to allow the steam to escape. Return to the oven for a further 2 minutes, allow them to crisp, then transfer to a wire rack to cool completely.

5 When ready to serve, pour 100ml (3½fl oz) cream into a saucepan and whip the remainder until just peaking. Pile into a piping bag fitted with a 5mm (¼in) plain nozzle.

6 Add the chocolate, butter, and syrup to the saucepan with the cream and heat very gently until melted, stirring frequently. Meanwhile, pipe cream into each choux bun and pile on to a serving plate or cake stand.

7 When the sauce has melted, mix well, and pour over the choux buns. Serve immediately.

serves 4

prep 30 mins, plus cooling • cook 30 mins

2 piping bags with a 1cm (½in) plain nozzle and 5mm (¼in) plain nozzle

freeze cooled and unfilled buns for up to 3 months; thaw before filling and serving

Pear and cinnamon strudel

Hailing from Austria, strudels encase fruit fillings in layers of flaky pastry.

INGREDIENTS
4 ripe pears, peeled and sliced
2 tsp ground cinnamon
handful of raisins
1–2 tbsp golden caster sugar
15 sheets filo pastry
knob of butter, melted, to brush

METHOD
1 Preheat the oven to 200°C (400°F/Gas 6). Line a baking sheet with baking parchment. Place the pear, cinnamon, raisins, and sugar in a bowl, mix well, then put to one side. Brushing the sheets of filo with a little melted butter as you go, layer 3 sheets on the baking sheet, then layer another 3 next to them.
2 Sit another 3 layers of filo pastry on top, placing them with the long edges facing in the other direction. Repeat with another layer of 3 so you have an oblong-shaped base. Spoon the filling down the centre, then fold over the edges. Top with a final layer of 3 sheets of filo and brush the whole thing with butter. Bake in the oven for 30–40 minutes, or until golden brown.

serves 4

prep time 10 mins
• cook time 40 mins

Crème pâtissière

A rich, sweet pastry cream used for filling fruit tarts and choux buns.

INGREDIENTS
300ml (10fl oz) milk
2 egg yolks
60g (2 oz) caster sugar
20g (¾ oz) plain flour
20g (¾ oz) cornflour
¼ tsp pure vanilla extract

METHOD
1 Pour the milk into a saucepan and heat it to simmering point.
2 Beat the eggs and sugar together in a bowl, mix in the flour and cornflour, then pour in the hot milk, and mix well.
3 Return the mixture to the pan and bring it slowly to the boil, stirring continuously until it becomes smooth and lump-free. Once the mixture reaches boiling point, reduce the heat, and simmer, stirring for 1–2 minutes, to cook the flour.
4 Allow it to cool a little, then stir in the vanilla extract. Use at once, or cover and chill until needed.

makes 300ml
(10fl oz)

prep 10 mins
• cook 5 mins

Florentines

These crisp Italian biscuits are packed full of fruit and nuts, and coated with a thin layer of luxurious dark chocolate.

INGREDIENTS

60g (2 oz) butter

60g (2 oz) caster sugar

1 tbsp clear honey

60g (2 oz) plain flour

45g (1½ oz) chopped mixed peel

45g (1½ oz) glacé cherries, finely chopped

45g (1½ oz) blanched almonds, finely chopped

1 tsp lemon juice

1 tbsp double cream

175g (6 oz) dark chocolate

METHOD

1 Preheat the oven to 180°C (350°F/Gas 4) and line 2 baking trays with greaseproof paper.

2 Put the butter, sugar, and honey into a small saucepan, and melt gently over a low heat. Then allow to cool until it is just warm. Stir in the next 6 ingredients.

3 Drop teaspoonfuls of the mixture on to the baking trays, leaving space between them for the biscuits to spread.

4 Bake for 10 minutes, or until golden. Do not let them get too dark. Leave them on the baking tray for a few minutes, before lifting them on to a wire rack to cool completely.

5 Break the chocolate into pieces, and put it into a heatproof bowl set over a pan of gently simmering water. Make sure the bowl is not touching the water. Once the chocolate has melted, spread a thin layer of chocolate on the bottom of each biscuit, and place, chocolate-side up, on the wire rack to set. Spread a second layer of chocolate over the first layer. Just before the chocolate sets, make wavy lines in it with a fork.

makes 16–20

prep 20 mins
• cook 15–20 mins

Spritzgebäck biscuits

These delicate, buttery, piped biscuits are based on traditional German Christmas cookies.

INGREDIENTS

375g (13 oz) butter, softened
250g (9 oz) caster sugar
few drops of pure vanilla extract
pinch of salt
500g (1lb 2oz) plain flour, sifted
125g (4½ oz) ground almonds
100g (3½ oz) dark chocolate or milk chocolate

METHOD

1 Preheat the oven to 180°C (350°F/Gas 4). Line 2–3 large baking sheets with greaseproof paper and set aside.

2 Place the butter in a large bowl and beat with a hand mixer or wooden spoon until smooth. Gradually stir in the sugar, vanilla extract, and salt until the mixture is thick and the sugar has completely dissolved. Gradually add two-thirds of the flour, stirring in a little at a time.

3 Add the rest of the flour and ground almonds and knead the mixture briefly on a work surface to make a smooth dough. Shape the dough into rolls and, using a cookie press or piping bag and star nozzle, squeeze 7.5cm (3in) lengths of the dough on to the prepared baking sheets. Bake for 12 minutes, or until lightly golden, and transfer to a wire rack to cool.

4 Melt the chocolate gently in a microwave or in a bowl over a pan of barely simmering water. Dip one end of each biscuit into the melted chocolate, returning to the rack to set. The biscuits can be stored in an airtight container for 2–3 days.

makes 45

prep 45 mins, plus cooling • cook 15 mins

cookie press or piping bag

Rich chocolate biscuits

Use good-quality chocolate and cocoa powder to make these biscuits really tasty.

INGREDIENTS

100g (3½ oz) butter, softened
50g (1¾ oz) caster sugar
125g (4½ oz) plain flour
25g (scant 1 oz) cocoa powder
melted dark chocolate or milk
  chocolate, to drizzle (optional)

METHOD

1 Preheat the oven to 180°C (350°F/Gas 4). Line 2 baking trays with baking parchment. In a bowl, mix the butter and sugar together with an electric hand whisk or mixer until pale and creamy. Sift in the flour and cocoa powder, and beat until the mixture comes together to form a dough. You may need to bring it together with your hands at the end.

2 Roll the dough into 16 walnut-sized balls and place them on the baking trays. Press the middle of each one with your thumb to flatten it, or use a fork, which will decorate it at the same time. Bake for 20 minutes, then transfer to a wire rack to cool completely. Drizzle over the melted chocolate (if using), and allow to set before serving.

makes 16

**prep 15 mins, plus
cooling • cook 20 mins**

**electric hand
whisk or mixer**

INDEX

A

almonds, ground
  Florentines 88
  Silesian poppy tart 64
  Spritzgebäck biscuits 90
amaretto: Mini chocolate nut
  pastries 60
Apple pie 72

B

Bake pastry blind 9
Banana cream pie 70
biscuits
  Florentines 88
  Rich chocolate biscuits 92
  Spritzgebäck biscuits 90
Blueberry cream cheese tart
  68
bread
  Brioche 20
  Chapatis 46
  Ciabatta 34
  Crumpets 30
  Crusty white loaf 25
  English muffins 38
  Ficelles 12
  Foccaccia 22
  Morning rolls 26
  Moroccan spiced flatbreads
    52
  Naan bread 50
  Onion and herb loaf 36
  Pitta bread 48
  Plaited loaf 18
  Rye bread 42
  Seven-grain bread 14
  Sourdough bread
    with fennel seeds 28
  Spiced fruit buns 40
  Walnut bread 16
  Wholemeal bread 33
Brioche 20
  Making brioche dough 7
bulgur wheat: Seven-grain
  bread 14

C

Cannoli 80
Chapatis 46

cheese
  Blueberry cream cheese tart
    68
  Cannoli 80
  Silesian poppy tart 64
chickpeas: Moroccan spiced
  flatbreads 52
chocolate
  Cannoli 80
  Florentines 88
  Mini chocolate éclairs 62
  Mini chocolate nut pastries 60
  Profiteroles 82
  Rich chocolate biscuits 92
  Spritzgebäck biscuits 90
choux pastry
  Crème pâtissière 86
  Profiteroles 82
Ciabatta 34
cinnamon: Pear and cinnamon
  strudel 85
condensed milk: Key lime
  pie 74
coriander: Moroccan spiced
  flatbreads 52
cream
  Banana cream pie 70
  Crème pâtissière 86
  Florentines 88
  Lemon tart 76
  Mini chocolate éclairs 62
  piping 11
  Profiteroles 82
  whipping 11
Crème pâtissière 86
Croissants 44
Crumpets 30
Crusty white loaf 25

D

digestive biscuits: Key lime
  pie 74
dough
  make brioche dough 7
  mix and knead yeast dough 6
dried fruit
  Plaited loaf 18
  Scones 58
  Spiced fruit buns 40

Drop scones see Scotch
  pancakes

E

éclairs, chocolate 62
eggs
  Lemon meringue pie 78
English muffins 38

F

fennel seeds: Sourdough bread
  with fennel seeds 28
Ficelles 12
filo pastry
  Mini chocolate éclairs 62
  Pear and cinnamon strudel 85
flatbreads
  Moroccan spiced flatbreads
    52
  Naan bread 50
  Pitta bread 48
florentines 88
Foccaccia 22
fruit loaf: Plaited loaf 18

G

ghee: Chapati 46
glacé fruits: Cannoli 80
golden syrup: Profiteroles 82

H

hazelnuts: Mini chocolate nut
  pastries 60
herbs: Onion and herb loaf 36

K

Key lime pie 74
Kneading dough 6

L

lemons
  Lemon meringue pie 78
  Lemon tart 76
limes: Key lime pie 74

M

Make brioche dough 7
Make pastry 8

maple syrup: Pecan pie 66
Marsala: Cannoli 80
meringue: Lemon meringue pie
  78
millet: Seven-grain bread 14
Mini chocolate éclairs 62
Mini chocolate nut pastries 60
Mixing and kneading yeast
  dough 6
Morning rolls 26
Moroccan spiced flatbreads 52
muffins: English muffins 38

N
Naan bread 50
Nut: Mini chocolate nut pastries
  60

O
oats: Seven-grain bread 14
onions: Onion and herb loaf 36

P
Pancakes, Scotch 54
pastries
  Cannoli 80
  Croissants 44
  Mini chocolate éclairs 62
  Mini chocolate nut pastries
    60
  Pear and cinnamon strudel
    85
  Profiteroles 82
pastry
  Apple pie 72
  baking blind 9
  Banana cream pie 70
  Blueberry cream cheese tart
    68
  decorating pastry 10
  Lemon tart 76
  making pastry 8
  Pecan pie 66
  Profiteroles 82
  Silesian poppy tart 64
  trimming 10
  see also choux pastry, filo
    pastry, shortcrust pastry
Pear and cinnamon strudel 85

pears
  Pear and cinnamon strudel 85
  Silesian poppy tart 64
pecan nuts: Pecan pie 66
pie *see also* tart
  Apple pie 72
  Banana cream pie 70
  decorating pastry 10
  Key lime pie 74
  Lemon meringue pie 78
  Pecan pie 66
piping 11
Pitta bread 48
Plaited loaf 18
polenta: Seven-grain bread 14
poppy seeds: Silesian poppy
  tart 64
Profiteroles 82

Q
quinoa: Seven-grain bread 14

R
raisins
  Pear and cinnamon strudel 85
  Plaited loaf 18
  Silesian poppy tart 64
rice, brown: Seven-grain bread
  14
rice, ground: English muffins 38
Rich chocolate biscuits 92
rosemary
  Foccacia 22
  Onion and herb loaf 36
Rye bread 42
rye flakes: Seven-grain bread 14

S
Scones 58
Scotch pancakes 54
semolina
  English muffins 38
  Silesian poppy tart 64
sesame seeds: Seven-grain
  bread 14
shortcrust pastry
  Apple pie 72
  Banana cream pie 70
  Lemon meringue pie 78

Silesian poppy tart 64
Sourdough bread
  with fennel seeds 28
Spiced fruit buns 40
Spritzgebäck biscuits 90
strudel: Pear and cinnamon
  strudel 85
sultanas: Scones 58

T
tart *see also* pie
  Blueberry cream cheese tart
    68
  Crème pâtissière 86
  decorating pastry 10
  Lemon tart 76
  Silesian poppy tart 64
techniques
  Bake pastry blind 9
  Make brioche dough 7
  Make pastry 8
  Mix and knead yeast dough 6
  Pipe 11
  Trim and decorate pastry 10
  Whip cream 11
Trim and decorate pastry 10

W
Waffles 56
Walnut bread 16
whipping cream
  Plaited loaf 18
  Whip cream 11
Wholemeal bread 33
wine: Cannoli 80

Y
yeast dough, mixing and
  kneading 6
yogurt
  Moroccan spiced flatbreads
    52
  Naan bread 50
  Rye bread 42

London, New York, Melbourne, Munich, and Delhi

Senior Editor Ros Walford

Editorial Assistant Shashwati Tia Sarkar

Designer Elma Aquino

Jacket Designer Mark Penfound

Senior DTP Designer David McDonald

Production Editor Kavita Varma

Indexer Dorothy Frame

DK INDIA

Editorial Consultant Dipali Singh

Designer Neha Ahuja

DTP Designer Tarun Sharma

DTP Coordinator Sunil Sharma

Head of Publishing Aparna Sharma

First published in Great Britain in 2012.
Material in this publication was previously published
in *The Cooking Book, 2008* and *Cook Express, 2009*
by Dorling Kindersley Limited
80 Strand, London WC2R 0RL

Penguin Group (UK)

Copyright © 2008, 2009, 2012 Dorling Kindersley
Text copyright © 2008, 2009, 2012 Dorling Kindersley

10 9 8 7 6 5 4 3 2 1
001-186461-May/12

A CIP catalogue record for this book is available from the
British Library.

ISBN 978-1-4093-7498-5

Printed and bound by Hung Hing, China.